*We need no wings to
go in search of Him,
but have only a place
where we can be alone—
and look upon Him
present within us..*

TERESA OF AVILA

The
HEART
of
PRAYER

LANA BATEMAN

COUNTRYMAN
®

Nashville, Tennessee

❖ TABLE OF CONTENTS ❖

I n 1996 I joined the team of Women of Faith. I loved the honesty and integrity of the speakers. I loved the clear message that God is the good news, we are not. But one of God's greatest gifts to me was when Lana Bateman joined our team. From the first moment I met Lana I knew I wanted to hang out with her. It was clear to me that when I was in Lana's presence I was overwhelmed with a sense of the presence of Christ. Lana taught me to be still before my Father and enjoy Him. Being her friend has changed my life. There are people we meet and look up to but never feel we will be like because they seem so removed from our human experience. Then there are people like Lana, who laugh and cry as we do and yet are so caught up in the life and love of Jesus that they inspire us to move in closer to His heart.

You will love this book. It will welcome you into a life of communion and worship and you will never be the same. Let the adventure begin!

Your sister,

Prayer is a gift given by our Father who longs to have His children come alongside as He exhibits His wonders and pours forth His grace in this world. Certainly God could do all things without our prayers, and yet He has chosen us to be the vessels through which He flows as He accomplishes many of His plans and purposes for mankind. What an honor He has given us!

What a call for us, too. As we move into the simplicity of prayer, we begin to experience the reality that we, His children, are both frail and glorious. We become aware of our frailty in finding ourselves totally dependent upon Him for direction in prayer. And we glimpse the glory He has invested in us (John 17:22) while we watch His hand move in answer to the petitions He Himself has placed within us.

My desire is that as you read the pages of this book you might enter the simplicity, joy, and rest of having learned to hear and pray the heart of God.

During my early years as a Christian I knew little about prayer. I had a very busy life with a job, husband, children, and little time to myself. The quiet moments I snatched here and there were devoted to reading Scripture and exploring this God to whom I now belonged.

As time passed, I looked at other Christians and assumed their methods of petitioning God must be the *best and only* way. Soon I began in earnest to emulate what I saw others doing. I read the Bible for thirty minutes each morning and prayed through a written prayer list for half an hour.

Gradually my prayer list grew, and I had to type it out to get it into a manageable form. One might think that I would feel fulfilled with such an investment in prayer, but my times with God grew more and more stale. Eventually my entire prayer life felt rote and empty. At this point God began moving on my heart. He impressed me to throw away my prayer lists, for He wanted to do a new and freeing thing in my prayer life. He then began walking me through the first elementary steps toward the simplicity and rest of what has become a *living prayer life*.

Through His written Word, and the inspiration of
His Holy Spirit, He was calling me to come to Him in a
new way. I was to wait upon Him to expose His heart
and desire concerning our time together. A whole new
world began opening to me as I entered the wondrous
place called the Heart of Prayer.

This book is based on my personal journey into
the Heart of Prayer. I am not a theologian. My formal
training is on my knees, not in a classroom. I don't
know all that your own, unique journey will be—all
I can do is share the peaks and valleys of mine—but
I do know that God wants you to make that journey
into His heart. My prayer is that by sharing what I've
learned, you'll be more encouraged, you'll trust God
to be with you each step of the way, you'll pray more
fervently, and you'll be more confident that God is
interested and involved in every aspect of your life.

*There are thoughts which
are prayers. There are
moments when, whatever
the posture of the body,
the soul is on its knees.*

VICTOR HUGO

CHAPTER ONE

UNDERSTANDING GOD'S SOVEREIGNTY

S uzanne stood waiting for me after I spoke at her
church's yearly women's retreat. The previous
hour I had shared the importance of understanding God's sovereignty in our lives, and I always
expect questions after such a topic.

In the moments that followed, I was thrilled to
hear not a question, but a beautiful testimony of God's
divine control in one of the most sensitive areas of her
life.

Suzanne and daughter Karen had spent years in a
strained relationship. Karen was described as an arro-
gant child who had everything she needed within herself; she found little use for others. She was strong to a
fault and a very unapproachable child. These issues

intensified as Karen entered her teenage years, and the crisis exploded when at the end of her freshman year in college she returned home to tell her mother that she needed money from her education fund to pay a large drug debt. Suzanne was devastated.

As Suzanne sought God, she felt He wanted her to take her hands off of Karen, trust her daughter to go to the rehabilitation meetings alone, and allow her to work this out on her own. While this is not the best way to handle all children with drug problems, for this particular child God's heart was for Suzanne to trust Karen even when it didn't appear she was worthy of that trust.

It was very difficult, for her mother's heart wanted desperately to control the situation. However, in spite of her natural desire to try to make things turn out well for her daughter, Suzanne didn't hover, constantly worry, or expect more than what she thought her daughter could give in terms of rehabilitation. In the next months, Karen successfully walked through the rehabilitation process, and her life took an obvious turn for the better. Out of something horrible, something good began to emerge.

Suzanne said that her unaffectionate, unapproachable daughter had somehow softened through the experience. Now her daughter freely hugged and kissed her when she came home or left the house. Some strange wall had come down, and a relationship between them became possible for the first time. She felt the Lord showed her that Karen had come face–to–face with the first thing in her life that she couldn't control and it had broken her will.

Suzanne said: "As you spoke today, I recognized God's sovereignty in allowing this thing to touch my daughter's life. No, it wasn't His perfect will for her, but He allowed it. What had seemed initially to be so totally devastating had changed her life and her inability to relate to others in a loving way."

Suzanne expressed that she would never view God's sovereignty in the same way again. What once was only a theological teaching, now had made a home in her heart.

An understanding of God's sovereignty is pivotal to entering the simplicity of prayer. How can we come to know the *rest* that exists in conversing with our Father if we do not grasp that He is in control of all things?

I recently taught a group of young people about the sovereignty of God. As the class began, there were grumblings and much discomfort about even broaching the subject. "Too much that can easily be misunderstood," said one. "Who can really get it?" added another. The concerns they voiced were not without merit. It's easy to rest in God's sovereignty and control when life is wonderful and the world is at peace. But what about the times when we are suffering and the world is writhing with unrest?

If I hadn't strongly believed in the importance of addressing this facet of God, I could have looked for something more agreeable to teach that group. However, with the tremendous freedom I have come to know through laying hold of the truth about God's sovereignty, I could not walk away without offering it to them even when they didn't know they needed it.

So, let's take a look at a part of our God that may revolutionize your approach and response to prayer.

In 1994 Dr. Frank Seekins wrote a book called *Hebrew Word Pictures*. In his book Dr. Seekins speaks of the fact that every Hebrew word has a definition, and that each letter in a Hebrew word is also a word picture and has a definition. By defining each letter within the word, and taking into consideration the root of the word, a phrase is produced that further clarifies the meaning of the word.

For instance, if we take the word *fear* in Hebrew, *Yearah*, and define each letter, considering the root of the word, we find the phrase, *to see the hand of*. In other words, to fear God we need to see the hand of God in all things—His sovereignty.

No wonder Israel's King David was a man after God's own heart, for you don't have to read far in the Psalms to see that David saw God's hand in everything. Yes, the Lord our God is not only God *of* all things, but God *over* all things. (Read 2 Samuel 16:1–11 to see David's response to His Lord in an abusive situation.)

Facing the terrible agony and inhumanity of the cross, how else could Jesus have prayed as He did in the Garden of Gethsemane? In essence, He was saying, "Father, this is what I desire. Let this cup pass from Me. I don't want to go through what is coming; however, not My will but Thy will be done."

You see, **Christ understood that the Father is always after the highest good.** Therefore, no matter what the cost, how unjust, how cruel, or how unfair it might appear, Jesus wanted the Father's will above His own. The Son of God could pray such a prayer because He knew the Father controlled all things. Regardless of what the enemy might try to do to Jesus, the Heavenly Father, who stood above and controlled all things, would only let the enemy go so far. Even in the midst of this horrible act, the Father called forth the highest good.

We see in the Old Testament (Job 1, 2) that Satan had to ask permission to lay even one finger on Job. Also, in the New Testament look at the Lord's words to Peter right before the Crucifixion: *"Simon, Simon, behold, Satan has demanded permission to sift you like wheat; but I have prayed for you, that your faith may not fail; and you, when once you have turned again, strengthen your brothers."* (Luke 22:31,32 NAS). The Lord made it clear that Satan was given permission to do as he asked, for Jesus said, ". . . **when you have turned again** . . ." meaning after you have endured the trial, turn and be a help to encourage and strengthen your brothers.

The point is clear, whether Old Testament or New Testament, the enemy cannot touch us without God's permission.

That raises other questions doesn't it? What about the terrible things happening around us today? Surely God can't be over all of these things? The psalmist tells us, *"God sat enthroned at the Flood, and the Lord sits as King forever."* (Psalm 29:10 NKJV). How shall we then come to peace with such a sovereign God? He desires peace and yet allows wars . . . He loves giving life and yet many die . . . He longs for kindness of heart and yet cruelty and violence abound.

While we will never have all the answers, I believe we can understand what is needed to bring us into a place of rest in prayer.

God sees the *big picture.* He never said He would stop the sin in this world that mankind chooses. He did, however, say that He would be with us no matter what . . . even in the midst of what sin might try to do to us.

God didn't spare Daniel the lion's den, but His angel was sent to close the mouths that would have destroyed Daniel. God was right there with him. The three Hebrew youths walked in the fiery furnace, but when those who sought to destroy their lives looked in, there were four in the flames. Jesus was right there with them.

God may purpose or allow us to go through terrible circumstances, but He will not abandon us through them. It is critical for us to know that it is not our God who chooses evil in this world, nor does He tempt us in any way. God is love, mercy, and holiness.

Why then does He allow such evil to touch our lives? Well, if He never said He would stop sin in this world, every human being will be touched by sin in one way or another. However, and this is important, God will not allow the struggle or pain to be wasted.

Satan has certain rights where this world is concerned, for the title deed fell into his hands when Adam and Eve sinned. Jesus described him three times as *the prince of this world* (John 12:31; John 14:30; John 16:11).

It will not always be this way; Christ will reclaim this world when He comes for us. Praise God, He is coming again!

Until then, what Satan uses to try to destroy us is being transformed in God's hand daily. Our Father will take our woundedness and draw from it those things which help fashion, strengthen and train us for all that He has purposed for us to walk in now and throughout eternity.

He also will take our sufferings and make them a precious treasure from which He will minister valuable riches of understanding, care, and compassion to the hearts of His other hurting children. Remember, God uses all things ultimately for His glory—even what the enemy means for evil.

For those who continuously harden their hearts against God, evil may be the discipline of a life devoid of the Life–Giver. When we do not belong to Christ, our lives are fair game for the enemy.

"How," you may ask, "can God allow such struggle and pain if He really loves us? I couldn't do that to my children." My best answer to that question, desiring not to minimize the cry of the heart, would be the following illustration.

When my sons were born, immunizations were given to infants at about six weeks of age. The shots were for diphtheria, tetanus, whooping cough, and polio. Each one of these conditions, if contracted, could be fatal. As a mother, I walked into the doctor's office and handed him my little newborn, allowing him to inject several needles with serum into my son's thigh.

If my baby could have spoken, in the midst of the screaming, he might have cried out: "Why have you done this to me? You have put me in the hands of a complete stranger and allowed him to bring the greatest pain into my life that I have ever known. How could you really love me and do this to me?"

Because I could see the horrifying possibilities that might mean death to my child later in life, I was willing to allow my baby to experience great pain in order to prevent potential destruction in the years to come.

Our Father is the greatest of all parents. He knows all things. He, too, is willing to allow us to know certain pain and struggles that we might be protected from greater ones as the years pass.

Perhaps this may seem a little simplistic, yet it is so important in beginning to understand that our God is in control. Nothing is out of His knowing, moving, or allowing on the face of this earth. We can rest, knowing that a God of love, justice, mercy, and longsuffering is at the wheel of this vessel we call life. He has even numbered our days. Psalm 139:16 (KJV) says:

> *. . . and in Thy book they were all written,*
> *The days that were ordained for me,*

When as yet there was not one of them.

David was saying that our days are written in heaven . . . all of them. You might say that *the fullness of our days is listed there.* When our days are complete, no one will be able to keep us in this life. Until then, one might say that we are immortal. The day is written.

Does this mean we are not to take precautions with our lives? Of course not. Through His Word the Lord constantly calls us to live wisely, but we should not live in fear of losing our lives. He wants us to be fully alive in this life until we finish our course and step into the next. Our day is written.

We should live each day fully as a part of the journey He has given us. One of the great gifts that comes through resting in God's sovereignty is a new heart–set. For when we see that He controls all things, every situation is an opportunity to look for what God has invested in that moment or in that struggle.

No more do we ask ourselves, "Why did I do something so ridiculous?" But rather, we turn to our Father and say, "You allowed this. What are You trying to show me, Lord . . . what are You trying to teach me . . . what do I need to see?"

Can you begin to see why understanding God's sovereignty can make prayer a place of rest? No matter what we ask, He abides over us *and* our prayers. A sovereign God reigns and longs to teach us to pray the desires of His heart even within the desires of our own.

Maintaining Personal Honesty

After building a prayer foundation by understanding God's sovereignty, we must commit that we will always, *always* come to Him honestly in our prayer times. He is not interested in pretense or denial. He is searching for honest hearts.

We must be willing to confess we are angry with Him when we are feeling that way. He is able to handle our anger, and He knows when it is there, whether or not we are honest about it. As Job went through his terrible trials—which Satan was allowed to bring into his life—he was understandably angry. He cursed the day he was born and the womb that bore him. Again and again he railed. But not until he admitted his anger and prayed for his friends did God turn his life around and restore one hundredfold all Job had lost. He had acknowledged and repented of his anger to God Himself, and then his life began anew.

Some people would tell you not to ask God questions like, "Why?" I am not one of those people. I believe that asking God "Why?" indicates that we have the faith to know that He, and only He, has the answer.

I believe "Why?" is a question that ultimately shows faith. However, once we ask the question, we must be willing to rest in His timing for the answer. For some situations the answer may come fairly quickly, for others, very slowly, and for some, not until we see Him face–to–face. If we trust in the sovereignty of our God, we wrestle our way to peace in the knowledge that if an answer is for our highest good, the God who loves us will not withhold it.

Honesty in our prayer time is critical. It opens the way for us to hear and respond to our Father in deeper and more profound ways. We must purpose in our heart to be open, honest, and transparent, resting in His sovereignty. Such a foundation for prayer will never leave us disappointed!

*If you lack knowledge,
go to school. If you
lack wisdom, get
on your knees.*

VANCE HAVNER

*In the silence and
purity of the heart,
God speaks.*

MOTHER TERESA

CHAPTER TWO

Preparing for Prayer

FINDING TRUE SOLITUDE

*But you, when you pray, go into your inner room, and
when you have shut your door, pray to your Father.*

MATTHEW 6:6 *NAS*

My "inner room" has always been the big
leather recliner in my living room. There
I have found a space that is restful and
peaceful. On winter mornings there is usually a warm
fire crackling next to me, and in the summertime the
sunlight floods through the windows just above me.
It is a wonderful place to have a quiet, intimate
conversation with my Father.

I call these meetings my "set aside" time for
prayer. While I find myself speaking to the Lord
throughout the day as I remember a prayer need, see

something beautiful, or just experience a sweet moment, the morning remains my special time.

Many believers have such life constraints that it is difficult for them to set aside times for prayer. For instance, a father who holds down two or three jobs certainly will find it difficult to have that special time, but he can talk to the Lord as his day progresses. A young mother might not have specific time with the Lord every day, but she can thank Him every time she sees her baby smile. She can talk to Him while grocery shopping or on those drives to and from work. Time with the Lord may differ because of circumstances, but He sees the heart and is pleased when we think of Him and speak to Him throughout our day.

For those who have the luxury of a special time with the Father, the most peaceful place for prayer may be in the bedroom or a small office. Others may seek the quiet of a corner in the family room or a comfortable chair in an empty guest room. Wherever you feel the most at ease, there you will find the perfect solitude for time with the Lord.

Setting aside a portion of the day also varies with each person. Some say that evenings offer the best privacy and alone time. Others can't imagine not meeting our sweet Friend in the early morning hours. Whatever works best with your lifestyle and its demands is just right for you.

Once you have carved out the right place and the right time, the first step toward a new and creative experience in prayer has been established.

EXPERIENCING PERSONAL WORSHIP

Our Heavenly Father desires to touch us with His presence so there can be a free flow between our related hearts.

Scripture indicates that every good thing comes from God and returns again to Him. This being so, then even worship and prayer must certainly originate with Him. In my personal prayer experience, I sensed that the Lord wanted me to come to Him constrained by love and not by duty or responsibility. All of the "shoulds" and "ought–tos" that had kept me rigid in times of devotion had to be thrown away. That process of personal change was a frightening time for me. He had to do a great work in my heart so I could long for Him and be drawn to Him by love rather than my own self–discipline.

In order to spend my energies doing what pleased God in my prayer time, I needed to know how *He* wanted me to worship and how *He* wanted me to pray.

Because God inhabits the praises of His people (Psalm 22:3), few things draw Him nearer than our praise and worship. God delights in teaching us different ways of worshiping Him so that our times together are filled with His creative touch. Worship comes before prayer, for it is worship that creates a profound connection between the two of us, better enabling the heart to pray the will of the Father.

"What kind of worship?" you might ask. I quickly found that there are a number of answers to that question. On different days, He led me in different ways. Everything was new. The old habits were gone, and now I sat before Him asking what would please Him rather than simply presenting to Him what I felt I should do.

One morning He stirred my heart as I listened to worship music. Line after line, I silently repeated each word. After a few songs, I began to sense His nearness and our hearts connected. Not until then was I ready to pray. On another occasion that connection came through His leading me to wave hand banners with my favorite worship music. This act of worship took me into a new realm. My whole being—body, soul, and spirit—reached up to bond with the heart of the Father.

I discovered that He had His own desires for our morning meetings, and I found that His ways were so much higher than my own. Every day was a new experience. At times I didn't feel His presence as much as I might have liked, but I soon realized that these were the times He tried my heart to see if I wanted to be with Him even when my feelings weren't engaged.

Perhaps one of the biggest surprises for me came when His Spirit simply asked me to sit and "do nothing." He just wanted to be with me. He wasn't interested in words or actions; He just wanted me to sit with Him and allow Him to wrap me in His presence.

Another way He impressed my heart to worship was by singing personal songs to Him. I am not a singer, neither am I one who can quickly rhyme words or compose melodies. In fact, I am one of the few who could be paid *not to sing*. My first grade teacher gave me a bird whistle to keep me from singing when the class sang choruses for our parents. However, I began trying to do what I believed He was asking. The results were astounding. Our time started by my making up a song about who He is. I sang of His wonderful creative power, His beauty, and His faithfulness. It was like expressing my delight in all that He is through a simple childlike song. Not a person in the world would care to hear such a rhyme-less, rhythmless song from me; thankfully, God's thoughts and God's ways are much higher than ours. As I sang, I immediately experienced His delight in what seemed so silly to me. I had never felt His presence bond so quickly to my heart.

I came to a sweet rest during those special times. All the cares and concerns seemed to drift away. Oh, it definitely took a while to adjust to not striving— we humans are so good at filling the silence to make ourselves more comfortable—but this new, personal way of being in God's presence always brought peace to what otherwise would have been a hectic day.

Many years ago I heard a pastor tell a story about an old monk who lived in a monastery in Europe. The old man sang the *Ave Maria* every Christmas Eve as the brothers celebrated the birth of Jesus. He had a very poor voice and even poorer pitch, but no one wanted to take the honor away from him. Year after year they endured as he awkwardly belted out one of Christendom's most beautiful hymns.

The old monk died shortly before Christmas one year, and a new young brother was asked to sing the traditional song of celebration. He was a highly gifted man who had been trained with the opera before taking his vows. A magnificent sound filled the abbey as the young monk began to sing. What exquisite beauty!

Shortly after midnight, it was said that an angel visited the abbot. "Why was there no song to the Christ Child tonight?" he asked. "No song!" responded the abbot. "Never has there been a more beautiful song sung to our Lord than what was performed this night." "No," said the angel, "the Father reads the heart, and there was no song for the Christ Child this year."

Like the old monk, we must be willing to sing in our quiet times no matter what the sound . . . for God delights in the songs of our hearts, especially when they are songs of worship.

God waits for us to put away our insecurities and self–consciousness so that we can come to Him as a child. Remember, He is the one who said: *"I tell you the truth; anyone who will not receive the kingdom of God like a little child will never enter it"* (Mark 10:15 NIV). Our God seeks those who will come into His presence with open hands, an open heart, and a desire to please Him no matter what He might ask. This is a heart ready to worship and ready to pray.

I cannot leave this chapter on *Preparing for Prayer* without sharing some thoughts on worship as it applies to walking through our everyday lives. The way we live can become a free–flowing act of worship. What better way to prepare us for a life of prayer?

A few years ago I was given a note written by Elaine Cook, a dear Bible teacher who lives in British Columbia, Canada. Elaine had gone to the Lord in her personal prayer time, asking Him to teach her how to worship Him *with her life*. As He began to impress her heart with His answer to that prayer, she wrote these words:

> *When you accept whatever situation you are in without murmuring, you are worshipping Me.*
>
> *When you can rejoice in Me in the midst of your infirmities, you are worshipping Me.*
>
> *When I have brought pressures to bear upon you to bring out the gold of My nature and you bear them patiently—blaming not Me, or another person, nor yourself, then you are truly worshipping Me.*
> *When you can "forgive yourself" for your weaknesses*

and failures and cease expecting your human nature to bring forth perfection, you are worshipping Me.

When you have come to the place of recognizing and acknowledging that "of myself I can do nothing," then do I have your praise.

When you can look upon a wasted life and agree that I can and will make this one every whit whole—that this is My desire—then you have offered Me true worship, for you have seen My true nature.

When you look upon My natural creation and the beauty of it and magnify Me, then am I worshipped.

When you hear My Word within you saying, "This is the way—walk ye in it" and you obey My Word with rejoicing, I feel worship from you.

When you look with compassion upon one who is afflicted, tossed, and broken, then am I worshipped. When you recognize My Body and honor them as My brethren, this is true worship unto Me.

When your lips are silent because of your pain, and you lift your heart to Me, I feel your worship.

When you say, "I cannot—please help me!" then am I worshipped.

Worship is a heart attitude in every place and situation in which you find yourselves. It acknowledges My Lordship, the righteousness of My nature, the truth of My Word, and the reality of My indwelling presence. You may offer true worship at all times and in every situation by keeping your heart right toward Me and toward your fellowman.

To worship the Father before prayer brings Him great joy, and to live a life of worship prepares us for the prayers of a lifetime! [1]

[1] Elaine Cook, www.kingdomgospel.org

The devil considers any real prayer dangerous.

CATHERINE MARSHALL

CHAPTER THREE

Purpose of Prayer

RELATING TO GOD

Prayer is the primary way in which God calls us to relate to Him. In prayer we converse with and worship our Father, we confess our struggles, express our needs, and intercede for others before His throne.

But prayer is much more. It is a time of *relationship*. God treasures this special bond with His people.

Perhaps one of the greatest purposes of prayer is to keep us in constant communion with our God, who desires to know and be known. Psychology tells us that one of the greatest needs of the human heart is to be known and accepted for who we really are. God, though His heart is far greater than a mere human heart, also desires to be accepted for who He is, not because He is some Santa Claus in the sky. No, He wants

45

us to accept all of *who He is* and enjoy Him for the good things as well as the things He allows to touch our lives that we don't understand. That is why we discussed sovereignty in the first chapter, and why that essential theme is woven throughout the pages of this book.

Some years ago I found myself hard–hit with multiple personal tragedies. I call it the time of the whirlwind, hurricane, and cyclone.

My mother–in–law, Aline, had become ill, but before she was diagnosed with terminal cancer I spent time in prayer for her recovery. The Lord's response to my prayers was, "No, she will not live. You just love her into My arms." God would really need to do a work in both of us to make that love possible, because my mother–in–law didn't like me and I responded by keeping my distance. However, during the months that followed the Lord worked on our relationship. He started drawing us together as He showed me how to woo her with kindness. Finally, the walls began to come down, and we dared to move toward each other.

During this time, my husband (her son) left our home after eighteen years of marriage. As his mother's cancer progressed, it became necessary for me to move in with Aline. Shortly before her death, she reached out for God. What I had dreaded became a great privilege and blessing, for the Father taught us mother–daughter love and intimacy —something neither of us had ever known. Yet, even as we drew closer to each other, God kept saying to my heart, "Lana, hold loosely to what you are experiencing, for just as it has come quickly, it will soon be gone."

Another surprise occurred during those final months with Aline. I began to have recurring dreams of childhood abuse. Graciously, God placed a wonderful Christian counselor in my life to help me face this new, but old issue. That time of counseling was deeply painful, and yet it bore great fruit in my life. Though I would never have asked for it, I certainly could see God's hand in what was transpiring.

Three major and exceedingly painful events, all at once, erupted in my life: God asked me to love someone who didn't even like me; my Christian husband left our marriage; and I experienced self–revelation of childhood abuse.

Aline died the end of July, and the following July her son, Marc, asked for a divorce. With my marriage over and my mother–in–law gone, I felt my life had become loose ends, so I took a trip to be alone for a time. I spent those days seeking the Lord and trying to make some sense out of what had happened the previous eighteen months. So much had changed in my life in such a short time.

As the Lord often speaks to me in poetry, I was not surprised to find myself writing a poem at the end of my days of solitude. This is the verse He gave and the poem that was written:

HIS WAY

"In the whirlwind and the storm is His way . . . "
NAHUM 1:3 (*NAS*)

I was barely back from the storm of Aline's
death when the hurricane attacked.
At the height of its fury, the winds and
rain of abandonment bent the tress of
my soul with sheet upon wild sheet of
pain and loss.

All the terror of being alone took over my
heart in a fearsome display of power.

But You, who balance all things well, would
not leave me lost in despair and once
again You touched me.
The mirror was shattered. Its power broken.

Now there is peace.
I can sit by the fire and watch the storm,
resting in Your arms.
For You stand guard against the elements,
Both terrifying
and yet awesomely beautiful.
You secure the borders of this house with unseen
power.

Is that the way You guard the boundaries
of my heart, dear Friend?
Christ Jesus the Lion,

Lord of the storm without,
Protector of peace within.

It wasn't difficult to love God when my life was in order, but could I continue to love a God who would allow these terrible things to happen? Could I say, *"Shall we accept good from God, and not trouble?"* (Job 2:10 NIV).

As I've reread that poem through the years, I've come to rest more and more in the knowledge that my God is in control and reigns over all things, whether it be the peace we feel or the storm that rages about us. Accepting it has brought me into a far more intimate relationship with Him. Only those who come to relate to Him and trust Him based upon His sovereignty are able to receive all of God—Lord over the good things and Lord over the painful things of life.

Relating to God isn't just accepting everything about Him; it also means that we are willing to spend time with Him. How shall a friendship grow if we don't have time with the One with whom we desire to be close? How shall we know what He desires of us if we do not talk with Him and listen to His heart?

When we move into prayer with the Father, we move into partnership with Him. If earthly partners never spend time together, the likelihood of success in their venture is severely diminished. The same is true in our heavenly partnership.

One of the ways He calls us to maintain our relationship with Him is by constantly seeking Him in regard to applying the principles of Scripture in our lives. For instance the verse, *"Honor your father and mother so that you will live a long time"* (Exodus 20:12 NKJV), appears to be black and white, all inclusive. However, there sometimes seem to be many *grays* in Scripture. How would God have me honor my parents if they were Satanists, versus honoring parents who are Christians?

The need is clear: We must go to the Lord and ask how to apply each principle in our situations. This keeps us constantly seeking Him for guidance. Staying in relationship with God is an important part of our journey with the Lord and it is *critical* to a life of prayer.

PARTNERING WITH GOD

Many of us think of partnering with God as it relates to supporting a ministry with our finances or with our prayers, but walking side–by–side with the Creator of the universe means much more than this. God has ordained that He will accomplish many things upon this earth through the prayers of His people. He has a plan, and He has chosen those who will partner with Him to bring forth His plan through prayer.

When we look at partnering in the natural realm, we see two or more who decide on an action and work together, using their abilities to make it happen. However, we are not limited to this earthly realm. In some cases our rewards may begin here on earth, but in all cases there will be heavenly reward for those who partner with God. Those who pray are credited alongside those who carry out the work.

For example, in a situation such as praying for someone's salvation, we may not be rewarded by witnessing the results of salvation in that person's life on earth, but we certainly will be rewarded in heaven when all things are revealed. Yes, God is a rewarder of His people.

Yet the reward is not the most exciting part of being God's partner. The most exciting part is realizing that the God of the universe desires to move hand–in–hand with frail human beings in carrying out His plans on earth. I don't know about you, but that idea takes my breath away. What are we human beings that He should give us such a privilege? What a wonder!

"What is man, that You should exalt him,
that You should set your heart upon him, that
you should visit him every morning?"
(Job 7:17,18 NKJV).

It's a humble heart that can hold fast to God's character, wait in desperation for His voice . . . and see miracles.

ALICIA BRITT CHOLE

CHAPTER FOUR

Principles of Prayer

PRAYING WITH PASSION

Dictionaries describe "passion" as intense emotion, sexual desire/love, or anger. Most of us have grown up with that definition. One of the most difficult issues with using the word "passion" is battling with the world's definition. The world's passion and spiritual passion are almost antitheses of each other.

That being so, we are going to look at spiritual passion and its fervent longing and desire for God and for that which pleases Him. Spiritual passion also could be considered a fervency or hunger to see Him as He really is and not through the eyes of human distortion.

David beautifully expressed his spiritual passion: *"As the deer pants for the water brooks, so pants my soul for You,*

O God. My soul thirsts for God, for the living God" (Psalm 42:1,2 NKJV). Wouldn't it be wonderful if we felt that deep longing, that passion, every time we sat down to pray?

Over the years I've learned that when we enter a new and creative time of conversing with God, He awakens a passion within us. Now, I'd like to say that this passion never wanes, but that wouldn't be true. The times and circumstances in our lives may preoccupy us and hinder our passion. At these times we need to be honest with our Father, such as confessing, "Lord, I don't even know how to really long for You and Your ways. Please teach me." Another time we might need to pray: "Lord, I'm not feeling a passion to know You lately. Forgive me if I've let the world turn my eyes from the sweetness of the time we can have together. Restore the passion to my heart and teach me how to more consistently walk in it."

The Father knows all the struggles and pressures that try to rob us of intimacy with Him. When we want to long for Him, even though we may not know how, it pleases Him to answer such a heartfelt and honest prayer. Passion is important to our prayer life. Passion is full of life and energy and is fully alive to the moment.

Many years ago, after watching a television movie, I was struck with the vast difference between worldly passion and the passion of the Father. I remember talking to the Lord about what I had seen and felt. The movie was a tragic story about a priest who fell in love with a woman in his parish. I felt such emptiness after seeing that story. As I sat before the Lord sharing my heart, His Spirit began to explain the emptiness I was feeling. He impressed on my spirit that I had seen a facet of human passion with its frailty, its unpredictability, its futility, and its often tragic end. Then I felt Him say, *"There is a passion without emptiness and pain. A passion that is higher and greater than anything this world has to offer. I long for My people to know this passion."*

The Lord impressed my heart that not only was spiritual passion the highest experience of true passion, but also that the believer's most beautiful song would come forth from his or her greatest pain. These, He said, were the two things I could learn from what I had seen, and these are understandings that I have brought with me through years of relationship with My Lord.

Recently I was attending the symphony in Kansas City with my friend Luci Swindoll. During our conversation she asked me what my favorite musical instrument might be. I was quick to answer, "The cello." When she asked why, I responded that the cello expresses a deep, passionate longing. It resonates the longing of my heart for God.

Passion is an important part of prayer. No wonder my old prayer times had been so dead . . . they were devoid of this life–giving facet of relating to God.

PRAYING WITHOUT PLEADING

When prayer first became an important part of my life, I had serious misconceptions. Much of what I had been taught did not serve me well.

One time when Jesus was teaching about prayer, He used the example of someone running to a friend at midnight and asking for bread to feed an unexpected guest. It seems the friend didn't even come to the door, but shouted from inside the house:

"Do not bother me; the door has already been shut and my children and I are in bed; I cannot get up and give you anything."

Jesus then said, "I tell you even though he will not get up and give him anything because he is his friend, yet because of his persistence he will get up and give him as much as he needs. And I say to you, ask, and it shall be given to you; seek, and you shall find; knock, and it shall be opened to you. For everyone who asks, receives; and he who seeks, finds; and to him who knocks, it shall be opened.

"Now suppose one of you fathers is asked by his son for a fish; he will not give him a snake instead of a fish, will

he? Or if he is asked for an egg, he will not give him a
scorpian, will he? If you then, being evil, know how to give
good gifts to your children, how much more shall your
heavenly Father give the Holy Spirit to those who ask Him?"

   —*Luke 11:7–13* (*NIV*)

   Until recently, I believed this passage meant that I
was to storm the gates of heaven for anything important
to me. However, the Lord showed me that this passage
was not a comparison, but a **contrast** between the ways
of the world and the ways of heaven. He spoke to my
heart, *"The friend who refused to get up unless hounded to*
death is a picture of how the world deals with human needs."
If we beg and make ourselves obnoxious, the chances are
better that we will finally have what we ask—that is the
world's way. Jesus then described the Father's way. Simply
ask and it will be given to you; seek, and you shall find;
knock, and it will be opened to you (Luke 11:9).

   My prayer life changed dramatically with this
understanding. I no longer come again and again asking
the same things of the Father. Unless He truly burdens
my heart to continue praying about a certain issue, I
pray, leave the matter with Him, and believe He will do
His best for me. I trust Him. I trust His heart.

It is important to mention that when I say sometimes God burdens my heart to continue to pray about a situation or need, it is He who presses my heart. It is not my emotions, a personal desire, or determination to get what I perceive I want or need.

Emotions can cause us to feel we *must* continue to pray for something. For instance, a mother might feel so guilty about the way one of her children is living (thinking her child-rearing might have helped produce an unpleasant or sinful situation) that she feels it is her duty to cry out to God constantly about the issue. Because she is not rightly dealing with her emotions, she has chosen the world's way to petition God. She has become the one who is beating on the thoughtless friend's door, pleading again and again for help

As we begin to grow in Christ, the way we approach Him starts to change. Hopefully, we begin to mature. Paul speaks to that maturity: *"I write to you, little children, because your sins are forgiven you for His name's sake. I write to you, fathers, because you have known Him who is from the beginning. I write to you, young men, because you have overcome the wicked one"* (1 John 2:12,13 NKJV).

I believe that we can apply this principle to prayer. We have the *little ones*, the immature. They are forgiven and aware of their forgiveness but haven't yet moved on to be overcomers. They represent those who beg and plead like a child in prayer.

Now, the *young men* have become overcomers. These represent those who have come to the knowledge of who they are in Christ, and the strength and power He has invested in them for His kingdom's sake. They represent those who are developing a passion for God and are walking as victors in this life. In prayer, they represent those who have come to know the power and privileges of belonging to God. They see the power of prayer. They are in a very active mode. They are the doers.

The *fathers*, however, are those who know God. In prayer, the fathers are those who have become one with God's sovereignty and have fallen deeply in love with Him. Their prayers are a time of sweetness, intimacy, friendship, listening for His voice, and resting in His love that purposes all things. This is maturity in prayer—knowing Him.

Our heart's desire is to attain fatherhood (or motherhood!) in prayer as we grow toward becoming the heart of God in prayer.

Praying From a Position of Rest

The mature ones of whom we have just spoken are people who pray from a position of rest. They are aware of God being in control of all things, certain that He loves them, and are totally convinced that He always chooses the highest good. This is not a faith that says, "I must have this thing, or that outcome," but a faith that says, "God loves me and wants to hear my heart, and He loves me so much that *He wants me to hear His heart as well.*"

These mature ones have experienced His heart and His love through His Word, through life experiences, and through prayer. So fully are they convinced of His intentions toward them that they are now able to put away all striving. Prayer to them has become a place of rest. They are, however, sensitive to a particular burden for ongoing prayer that the Lord might desire in certain situations. (Example: In Isaiah 62:7 the Lord asks that we remind Him and give Him no rest or peace until He makes Jerusalem a praise in the earth.) Apart from these special prayer burdens, the mature ones rest in God's presence. With trusting hearts they leave all with Him, in Him, and to Him. He promised, *"Ask, and it will be given to you"* (Luke 11:9). They have asked. They will be given.

Our Heavenly Father longs for us to come into maturity . . . the *rest* of prayer. The longing heart, moving into this rest, will know it has at last come home . . . home to a whole new peace and freedom from the bondage of a begging, pleading prayer life.

The fewer words

the better prayer.

MARTIN LUTHER

CHAPTER FIVE

Personal Listening Prayer

EXPECTING GOD TO SPEAK

Imagine sharing your heart with someone you love. You start by telling them how much you love them, you express your joy at all the wonderful things they have brought to your life, and you continue by sharing your intimate longings and struggles. You have opened your heart to this dear friend—even your desire to be a better friend—but in response to all you have said there is nothing but silence. After a while you leave, but something is missing. The one you love says nothing.

Most of my early years of walking with Christ seem much like the encounter just described. I was never told that God wanted to converse with me and that He actually would speak in the stillness of my heart. But now I know how He delights in speaking into our thoughts, for He desires a genuine interchange with us.

Love gives and takes. Love expresses its heart. Love desires to hear what the other has to say. Just as you and I desire real communication with our children, our dearest friends, or our companions, so God desires to communicate with us. Why don't more people give Him that opportunity? Most of us were taught that God responds only through Scripture or through what our circumstances show us. But recent Bible studies and books—such as *Experiencing God* by Henry T. Blackaby, *God Calling* by Two Listeners, and *The Purpose–Driven Life* by Rick Warren—have prompted Christians to think they might have missed something incredible. As one who has learned to hear God speak, I can honestly say, "They have."

Listening to God speak begins with believing that He desires to speak to you, and that when given a chance, He will. Expecting God to converse with us is not pride, it is faith . . . and it is a faith that God honors.

KNOWING GOD'S VOICE

At first I was afraid to listen for God's voice. I was convinced that if I allowed thoughts to invade my mind during prayer, I would surely be making up "what I imagined I heard."

I am thankful that God's love is greater than our fear, and He will break down the walls to help us hear His voice even when we're insecure.

One of my very first prayers as a believer in Christ was that God would speak to me face–to–face, like a man speaks to his friend—the way He spoke to Moses in Exodus 33:11. However, my fear of "not doing it right" kept me paralyzed for some time. What if I made it up? Why would God speak to someone like me? Fear. Fear. Fear!

The veil of separation between God and man was destroyed at the crucifixion; the Father now calls us to come freely into His presence. With this in mind, I began to think, "Perhaps hearing Him speak might now be possible for all of His children."

As God began speaking to me, I came to understand three simple principles for knowing His voice. Perhaps these principles will lessen the anxiety of someone who is just beginning to experience listening prayer:

1. What God speaks is always edifying to His child. It will build you up, encourage you, and show you something you need to see in yourself, or teach you forgiveness.

2. What God speaks will always be spoken out of love and will produce forgiveness, restoration, or loving correction.

3. Nothing God asks will contradict or violate Scripture, His revealed Word.

HEARING GOD'S VOICE

L istening for God's voice is not just listening with your ears—it's listening with your whole being—and it's not for the faint of heart. Maybe you've been burned when you've mistaken something else for His voice. Maybe you've strained to discern Him for years, but He seems silent to your pleas for intimacy. Or maybe you already know the joy of His voice in your life. As you continue reading this book, you might be hesitant to try the paths I've walked in prayer. That's okay. You have your own unique, blessed journey deeper into the Father's heart—all that matters is that you stay faithful to the path He has appointed for you.

One day as I was praying, I felt the Lord impressing me with the words, "Try Me. Just try Me." I knew He was talking about listening prayer. I had grown to desire this interchange so badly that I finally was ready to risk being wrong. After I worshiped the Lord, telling Him what a delight He is to me and what an awesome God He is, I told Him everything that was on my heart. Then I reminded Him of the Scripture He had impressed on me the night before.

Saul was to be anointed as the first king of Israel, and yet he was fearful. He spoke of what a nobody he was, from a small tribe and one of the least of families. Samuel was unmoved by Saul's words and went on to anoint him as king. Samuel assured Saul, *"Do whatever your hand finds to do, for God is with you"* (1 Samuel 10:7 NIV). It was as if Samuel was responding to Saul's doubts with, "None of those things matter anymore. God is with you!"

I told the Lord that I knew He was speaking this to my heart, and at last I acknowledged my belief that He wanted to speak to me.

My first action of faith was to sit with a piece of paper in front of me. If I was expecting Him to speak, I needed to be ready. For some time I sat there and nothing happened. Then I felt He was saying, "Start by writing the words, 'My Child.'" Soon other thoughts began to come. These were some of His first words to me:

My Child,

Long I have waited for the fulfillment of My heart's desire to speak to My people . . . to find a place in your heart. Now, you have entered a new beginning. New life will swallow up death in you.

You speak of delight in Me. Before you even desired Me, I delighted in you! Your sweetness came before Me, and My love consumed you. You can only bear the manifestations of My love in small ways. I am creating in you an enlarged capacity to receive and experience even more. The best is yet to be.

Believe Me for great things. Do not be afraid to believe. I am not an earthly father who has favorites—or who fails his children. Dare to believe, and out of you will flow a river of My Spirit—a flood of the manifestations of your God. Hold fast! Believe! You shall not be disappointed.

I am not disappointed in you.

As I read what I had written, I was filled with awe. These were not words I would have spoken to myself. I am not, nor have I ever been, that kind to myself.

Later that week as I prayed, I remember talking to the Lord about my cat, Mesha. He is such a beautiful creature, and I was so thankful to have such a loving animal. While I addressed many other things in prayer, this was what I sensed the Lord saying after I prayed:

My Little One,

I will teach you the lesson of the cat you love. He fills a very special place in your heart, does he not?

So it is with My love for you. No one can take your place. No one can even come near. There is only one of you . . . I made no other. Just as none could ever be like Mesha to you, none can ever be like you to Me. Can you see it? Can you understand it? It is true. It is one of My great truths for your life. Don't ever allow it to leave your heart.

Rest in My love . . . My boundless love. I look upon you and see My very heart. Oh, that you might be able to rest in the depths of such love—free at last from all striving, free to simply "be" in Me. I wait for that sweet repose, for it delights My heart. You desire to bless Me—then rest in Me as the cat you love rests in you. Rest in Me.

God's words can be very encouraging when we allow Him to speak. One morning I had been asking His forgiveness for my critical response to something the night before. I was distraught that I had said such words. This is how I heard the Lord speak to that issue:

My Child,

All that you say is true, yet I do extend forgiveness. Notice that I say "extend," for while I freely give it, you must take it. Do not stay long in this place. Once you have faced the truth, and brought the offense to Me, you must move on for the time is short.

Do not be constantly evaluating your life for Me. It is in those things you do not calculate that I manifest the kingdom in you. It is not in what you try to do, but in what you allow Me to do through you. Trust that I will rise up in you. Trust. Trust. Trust!

God is very creative in listening prayer, just as He is in the ways He may ask us to worship Him. He even speaks to us powerfully through nature.

One of my favorite conversations with God took place on a ministry retreat. About a dozen of the prayer directors from Philippian Ministries went with me to Buena Vista, Colorado, where we spent five days in a cabin. What a glorious place! Majestic mountains, a rushing river, and wildlife everywhere. The morning after our arrival, the Lord had us go out into nature for devotional times alone with Him. I soon found myself beside a quiet pool where a family of beavers had built a dam. While listening to a tape of a magnificent Vivaldi symphony, I looked around and noticed the damage the beavers had done to the forest. My heart cried, "Lord, the beaver builds wonderful homes, but must the process leave such devastation? Must there be so many of these unsightly teeth–etched stumps among the beautiful trees?" I hardly finished speaking before He answered:

The rest of the trees you see are more beautiful because this little creature removed some. Out of this destruction that you think so needless, his magnificent home is built, and the seemingly disfigured remains show the thinning of My forest. The living trees are now more beautiful because others have been removed.

So it is with you, My child. There are things within you that appear to be good, but need to be removed so that what is left can be more beautiful and useful to Me. What the human perceives as good is often only a distortion. By My Spirit and your yieldedness, these distortions are exposed and removed. It is only then that the soul's beauty can be seen by the fullness of My light. Fear not the process. Like the beaver, keep your eyes and heart on the home and the beauty that surrounds it.

This little creature's abode is a fortress of power, for it can change the flow of a river by divine decree. Like Me, this particular home is not comely, that looking upon it you should desire it, but oh the wisdom hidden therein.

Safe and secure My little one lives, firmly planted in the midst of a raging river, totally unmoved by the dangers that surround, unconcerned about possible floods, unafraid of what could become of his little ones or his home should the waters swell and dismantle his place of security.

How differently he would build his home were it built upon fear. Would he build upon the main stream or the fast flowing river with its power and majesty? Would he build near the raging rapids? I think not.

Why do you suppose I planted this little one here? This furry character, insignificant among the giants of My wilderness, is a living testimony to My care, and a picture of you, My Little One.

The place I have called you to live is not comely that many should desire it. There will be some destruction of self to create it, but all that is left shall burst forth with a beauty that only the touch of My glory can explain.

Your new home is in a rather precarious place. A mighty river comes against it and flows around it, and yet the river itself must turn in the face of it, to shift the waters that would normally destroy.

Fear not a coming flood or sudden chaos, should giant tress fall near your resting place. For few in all of nature are more secure, even in the face of disaster, than those who live in the hollow of My hand in dangerous places.

Greet every day with joy as you survey the divine adventure in which I have placed you. Fear not, My Child, for I have caused King River to step aside that your abode should stand, and the floods you fear, these too are in My hands.

Fear not, for today is yours and Mine. You rest secure today, and if tomorrow brings a dangerous swell, then by the power of My right arm you shall prevail.

Some, terrified, will build their homes in rocky caves. No light or living water dances there. The darkness swallows up one's joy of life, and yet the heart shouts, "Here I am secure."

Perhaps you think My tender call will stop if you have chosen caves instead of streams. How little you know the God of grace and love. For you will hear Me reaching out for you among the rocks and cliffs you thought secure.

My wooing song will echo tenderly through breezes in the trees and morning stars. The darkness of the cave cannot defeat the distant call of rivers rushing by. Fear not. My songs are not for deafened hearts, but for frightened children, fearful of My love and what it asks.

The river calls and one day very soon you'll meet Me there. And at the river's edge we will rejoice, for it is in this

strange, precarious place, the mystery of My peace will build
your home. Here light and water play outside your walls,
and rivers move aside at My command. The raging floods
cannot destroy you there. Though natural eye would say it
isn't wise, the heart of God prepares this home for you.

One day when darkness seems to overcome, you will
respond to all My longing calls, and you will deem the river
safer still than the solid rock you called security.

The river calls, Beloved Child of Mine. Fear not, for
very soon you'll meet Me there.

This was the longest response the Lord had ever
given me, and it was an important one. It helped to
open my heart to ask a difficult thing, because that day
I asked the Lord to bring any and everything into my
life that might make me all that He wanted me to be.

Within two years, the stormy season of which I
wrote earlier struck my life. The Father was preparing
me with His love and hope. Though His words didn't
take the pain away, I could look back and see that He
was fully in control of my life, and these events were
no surprise to Him. He knew what was coming. How
I thanked Him for giving me those words before the
storms occurred!

God loves to speak to His people! What He says to each one of us may be expressed differently—He writes His words on human hearts, and we discern through our own personality and ways of expression—but be assured, He *will* speak if we will but risk asking and waiting on Him. Do I wait for the Lord to speak every time I am with Him? No, but when I do, I am encouraged, I am uplifted, and I am more prepared for this journey called life. Listening prayer is a treasure for every believer to experience. It is another valuable facet of relationship with our Father. I wouldn't want anyone to miss it. Will you risk the adventure?

*Any concern too small
to be turned into a prayer
is too small to be made
into a burden.*

CORRIE TEN BOOM

Prayer is not conquering God's reluctance, but taking hold of God's willingness.

PHILLIPS BROOKS

CHAPTER SIX

Pitfalls to Prayer

AVOIDING PRIDE AND DISOBEDIENCE

O ur God delights in humility, and He hears the prayers of the humble. *"If my people, who are called by My name, will humble themselves and pray and seek My face and turn from their wicked ways, then will I hear from heaven and will forgive their sin and will heal their land"* (2 Chronicles 7:14 NKJV, emphasis mine).

Because humility is the opposite of pride, it is no surprise that our Lord would make it a prerequisite to prayer, for God hates pride. One verse of Scripture that speaks powerfully regarding the issue of prayer and humility is: *"Then [the angel] said to me, Do not be afraid, Daniel, for from the first day that you set your heart on understanding . . . and on humbling yourself before your*

God, your words were heard, and I have come in response to your words" (Daniel 10:12 NAS). In this passage God teaches us two very clear principles of prayer. The first is that answered prayer often comes as a result of our desire to understand, and the second is the need for our willingness to humble ourselves before God.

God grants a great reward to those who walk in humility. *"I lead the humble in justice, and I teach the humble My way"* (Psalm 25:9 NAS). Isn't that the heart cry of those who love Him? Understanding the ways of God begins with a humble heart. *"To fear the Lord is to hate evil; I hate pride and arrogance"* (Proverbs 8:13 NIV). *"When pride comes, then comes disgrace, but with humility comes wisdom"* (Proverbs 11:2 NIV).

Pride speaks another language. Pride says, "Don't you know who I am?" Or, "You owe me." The language of humility says, "Father, here I am. Do with me as you please."

Lest we think this issue might not be a trouble spot for every one of us, perhaps we had better remember that the first great sin was committed in pride. Lucifer fell from heaven because he wanted to be exalted like the Most High God. Pride is such an insidious sin that I often wonder if all sin does not somehow find its roots there.

For those who desire an intimate prayer life, a humble heart paves the way. A humble heart is the *only* way. That is why I begin my time with the Lord by asking for a fresh cleansing of my heart. We never know when pride, disobedience, or unforgiveness may be trying to take up residence even in subtle ways. Far better to confess our failings and ask for cleansing than to risk missing true intimacy with our God in prayer. *"But your iniquities have separated you from your God; Your sins have hidden His face from you, so that He will not hear"* (Isaiah 59:2 NIV).

It is true that our *eternal forgiveness* was taken care of at the cross, but we continue to walk in a sinful world where our feet will get dirty along the way. When our Lord sought to wash Peter's feet, this is what transpired:

Then He came to Simon Peter. And Peter said to Him, "Lord, are You washing my feet?"

Jesus answered and said to him, "What I am doing you do not understand now, but you will know after this."

Peter said to Him, "You shall never wash my feet!"

Jesus answered him, "If I do not wash you, you have no part with Me."

Simon Peter said to Him, "Lord, not my feet only, but also my hands and my head!"

Jesus said to him, "He who is bathed needs only to wash his feet, but is completely clean; and you are clean . . ."

(John 13:6–10 NKJV)

Jesus was making it clear that Peter had already bathed (cleansed unto salvation), but he was walking in a dirty world and would need to come to his Lord for touch–ups along the way. He went further to indicate that Peter would have to let the Lord keep his feet clean if he wanted to *partner* with Him in this world. Now that got Peter's attention. What a picture: when we recognize that we have fallen short of God's great love for us, we confess our sin, and then thank Him for His forgiveness. A cleansed heart is a heart ready to pray.

Another barrier to a fruitful prayer life is disobedience. When we know what God wants and we choose to disregard it, then we are walking in disobedience.

Many years ago, Marty, a young singer from Arizona, came to me asking for emotional healing prayer. He was a macho–type man with thick gray hair and a prematurely gray beard. Marty had been a believer just a few years and was realizing that his woundedness was keeping him from going on with God. After a short visit, we scheduled a prayer time together. When we walked through Marty's life in prayer, I saw God do a tremendous work of freedom. Old wounds were touched and healed, tremendous pain was released, and Marty had a brand new beginning.

Only two weeks later, I received a call from him. He was sobbing, "I don't know what is the matter with me. I'm falling apart."

I quickly prayed and asked the Lord how to respond to him. My next words were, "Marty what is God asking you to do that you are not doing?"

His response was, "God is asking me to get out of this house and to quit using this woman I've been staying with. But, I'm not going to do it. God is asking too much!"

God had done something special in Marty's life through that special prayer time a few weeks earlier, but it would be two more years before this young man would experience the freedom God had accomplished for him. It took that long for Marty to set his heart to obey God. Until he was ready to obey God's voice, he would not see the benefit of God's healing touch in his life, nor would He discern God's voice so clearly again.

The same is true of prayer. God desires an obedient heart. Why should He bother speaking to us if we are not willing to obey? The sin of disobedience separates us from the power of prayer. Until we set our heart to obey, chances are we will not hear His voice. A prayerful heart is always willing for God to reveal issues of pride or disobedience in order that we might ask forgiveness and once again be restored to that sweet relationship for which our heart yearns.

RESOLVING UNFORGIVENESS

O
ne of the women involved in the Women of Faith conferences, who graciously allowed me to share her story, spoke of how she had harbored a quiet anger and resentment in her heart toward the father of her children. He had left her when their three girls were very young, and she had to fend for herself and her little ones, often not even having enough food on the table.

By the time she was thirty years old she had received Christ as her Savior. She desired a deeper relationship with her Lord, but something stood in the way. For almost a year she cried out to the Father. During this time it seemed like the windows of heaven were closed to her. At last, in desperation, she cried, "Lord, change me. The problem must be in me. Please change me." That was the prayer He had been waiting for. As He began to reveal the wounds of her heart, one of the first things He moved her to do was to contact her ex–husband and ask his forgiveness. At first she was incensed. "Ask *his* forgiveness," she thought, "after all he did to me?"

Finally, her desire for a closer walk and a tender prayer relationship with the Lord became greater than her desire to withhold forgiveness from this man who had brought so much pain into her life. She surrendered her determination to hold him accountable, humbled her heart before God, and talked to the father of her children. She told me: "I never felt freer than when I walked away from that encounter. I knew I had been obedient to the Lord. My ex–husband was stunned as I asked for His forgiveness for the hatred and resentment I felt for him through all those years. I forgave him for not being a father to our girls and for abandoning me to handle such responsibility. He was dumbfounded. He didn't know what to say to me. At last, he muttered, 'Sure I forgive you.' and it was finished."

Her relationship with the Lord took a turn that day. She found a sweetness in prayer and a depth of His presence she had not known before.

Oh, the power of forgiveness! It is so important to our Lord that He speaks about it to those who want to give tithes and gifts to God: *"Leave your gift there in front of the altar. First go and be reconciled to your brother; then come and offer your gift"* (Matthew 5:24 NIV).

CONTAINING THE WANDERING MIND

Some people have less ability to fully concentrate than others. Containing wandering thoughts is an ongoing struggle for me, as I have battled ADD (attention deficit disorder) all of my life. But God certainly sees and knows our hearts. He is patient with us and does not judge us for our straying focus.

The key, however, is not to give in to the wandering thoughts. We must not get up and walk away from our times with the Lord because of the battle within our minds. Rather, we must work around it.

I like to keep a little voice recorder beside the chair where I spend time in prayer. When "tyrannies of the urgent" distract me, I record notes to myself: "Call the exterminator." "Pay the bills today." Or "clean the garage by Friday before guests come." Any wandering thought goes straight to the electronic to–do list. By clearing the racing issues of my mind, I am more able to keep my heart turned toward God.

If other thoughts begin to invade, such as concerns over family members, I immediately turn those thoughts into prayer. I ask the Lord how best to pray for those people, and then I immediately pray. Perhaps the Lord allowed the thoughts to come, not to interfere with our time together, but rather to be sure the prayer He desires might be offered on that one's behalf.

If a random thought is clearly not a part of my to–do list and obviously not a call to prayer, then I treat it as interference from the enemy who does not want me to have intimacy with the Father. When those stray thoughts come, I quickly remind the enemy that my God is patient and kind and filled with understanding for my wandering mind. I acknowledge this as yet another opportunity to praise my Father. Our adversary doesn't like to be a facilitator of praise for his holy Opponent. My words of praise sting and cause him to pause his efforts to disrupt. However, if the battle still continues, I have found that pausing to sing a short song to the Lord helps to refocus my mind and draw me right back into His presence.

Remember, the battle is for the mind. We give it to the Lord in prayer, and we ask Him to protect it. This is not an occasion to "beat ourselves up" because we don't feel we are "doing it right." Rather it is a time to be aware of how graciously God accepts us even in our weaknesses, and how quickly He forgives and shows us ways to continue to draw near to Him in prayer.

*When thou prayest,
rather let thy heart be
without words, than thy
words without heart.*

JOHN BUNYAN

CHAPTER SEVEN

Promises of Prayer

BELIEVING GOD'S WORD

Believing God's Word is a critical part of the foundation needed to pray effectively. We must first trust that the God who spoke the Word is filled with love for us, desires only our very best, and will not grant our desired answer if doing so will be destructive to us somewhere down the line.

God takes all things into consideration. For instance, when you pray for a friend or loved one, He considers whether your request, when answered, would be the highest good for you, for the person for whom you are praying, and for all others involved. He carefully weaves all of these motivations together to produce the right answer at the most timely moment. All of this takes us back to the sovereignty of God. Do we want

His absolute best? Do we believe those things He has spoken are really true?

First, we must believe that He loves us:

"This is love: not that we loved God, but that he loved us and sent his Son as an atoning sacrifice for our sins" (1 John 4:10 NIV).

"Dear friends, since God so loved us, we also ought to love one another" (1 John 4:11 NIV).

"If anyone acknowledges that Jesus is the Son of God, God lives in him and he in God. And so we know and rely on the love God has for us. God is love. Whoever lives in love lives in God, and God in him" (1 John 4:15–16 NIV).

Secondly, we must believe that He sees and will bring to pass all of those things that are important in our lives.

"The Lord will accomplish what concerns me" (Psalm 138:8 NAS).

"Being confident of this very thing, that He who has begun a good work in you will complete it until the day of Jesus Christ" (Philippians 1:6 NKJV).

Our God is sovereign over every detail of life. He loves us and will accomplish everything that is important for us. What a wonderful foundation upon which to pray! Do we believe His Word? His heart is for our good. He will not withhold His best from us.

"Those who seek the Lord shall not lack any good thing" (Psalm 34:10 NKJV).

"For the Lord God is a sun and shield: the Lord will give grace and glory: no good thing will he withhold from those who walk uprightly (Psalm 84:11 NKJV).

Some might say, "If God desires only good things for me, then why doesn't He give me what I asked?" To this question I would respond, "Perhaps we don't always know what "good" means." From our perspective, "good" may mean just what seems or feels good at the time we are praying. From God's perspective, "good" means His very best. If we could see the whole picture, we would want nothing less.

APPLYING GOD'S WORD

Applying God's Word regarding prayer begins with looking at His promises on the subject and then seeing them within the full context of Scripture. Two of the most widely expressed verses on prayer are:

"Therefore I tell you, whatever things you ask when you pray, believe that you receive them, and you will have them" (Mark 11:24 NKJV).

"And whatever you ask in My name, that I will do, that the Father may be glorified in the Son" (John 14:13 NKJV).

I believe we must understand several principles when we apply God's promises of praying in belief and asking in Christ's Name.

First, we must pray what we understand to be the will of the Father (in Scripture), or what He directly reveals to us (when He speaks to us individually).

For instance, we know from Scripture that it is within the will of the Father for us to pray against adultery. Praying for someone's salvation is clearly encouraged in Scripture as well. Throughout the New

Testament we are told that His desire is that all come to a saving knowledge of His Son; therefore, we don't have to wonder if it is God's will for us to pray for another to receive Christ. We don't have to wonder if we should pray for the release of another soul from some great bondage like alcoholism, drugs, or prostitution. God clearly reveals His heart throughout His Word. His love longs for those who are bound to be set free. So, you can be sure that prayers for deliverance are within the will of God.

At other times, the Lord may impress your spirit and call you to pray specifically for a certain person or situation. We can know this type of prayer is God's will because He Himself instigated the prayer.

I remember in the 1970s passing a small hotel on my way to work at American Airlines. One day a new sign above the hotel proclaimed that every room had X–rated television. I was sickened. Every time I passed through the area and my eyes fell upon that sign, I felt His call to pray about that hotel. To my surprise, the hotel went out of business in about six months. I say "to my surprise" because I was a new believer and found myself often amazed at how God sometimes answered prayers so clearly.

TRUSTING GOD'S HEART

J esus will always be our best example of how to
pray. Let's look at two of His prayers.

First, He gave us the Lord's Prayer in response
to His disciples asking, "How shall we pray?"

*"In this manner, therefore, pray: 'Our Father in heaven,
hallowed be Your name. Your kingdom come. Your will be
done on earth as it is in heaven. Give us this day our daily
bread. And forgive us our debts, as we forgive our debtors.
And do not lead us into temptation, but deliver us from the
evil one. For Yours is the kingdom and the power and the
glory forever. Amen'"* (Matthew 6:9–13 NKJV).

Notice that there is no pleading; the prayer
simply asks for each thing and trusts the Father to
answer. The prayer begins with worship. *Father, holy
is Your Name.* After worship, there is a call for God's
kingdom to come and for His will to fill the earth just as
it fills heaven. Next, personal needs are addressed. *Give
us our daily bread. Meet our most basic needs, Lord. Then,
forgive us just as we forgive others. Don't bring us into
situations that tempt us to grieve You, but deliver us from the
evil one who desires to see us fall and sin against our God.*

These are the elements we see in the Lord's Prayer: worship, acknowledging God's will as the highest and best, personal requests, asking for forgiveness and cleansing, and seeking protection against evil. God knows that each of these is important to the human heart because of who we are and because of the world in which we live.

Jesus' last prayer before He faced the cross— as He knelt in the Garden of Gethsemane—also is a critical prayer for us to examine.

"O My Father, if it is possible, let this cup pass from Me; nevertheless, not as I will, but as You will." . . . Again, a second time, He went away and prayed, saying, "O My Father, if this cup cannot pass away from Me unless I drink it, Your will be done" (Matthew 26:39,42 NKJV).

In this prayer of Jesus, we see the most powerful of all principles of prayer and the greatest prayer to which we can attain. While we may ask for what we desire—and we should always feel free to do so—ultimately, we must seek the Father's will above anything we might want or ask. This prayer is from the Son to the Father. It is every bit *God's prayer to God.* In the very heart of prayer, we find God's prayer, and in God's prayer we will never be disillusioned.

There are two kinds of people:
those who say to God,
"Thy will be done," and
those to whom God says,
"All right, then, have
it your way."

C. S. LEWIS

Prayer does not change God, but changes him who prays.

SOREN KIERKEGAARD

CHAPTER EIGHT

Privileges of Prayer

EXPERIENCING ANSWERED PRAYER

One of the greatest privileges of prayer is receiving God's answers. Although many answers are clear from the beginning, others may come after a waiting season. Yet others may even draw us right into a miracle.

Some years ago I heard an account of just such prayer. Dr. Newman Hall, while vacationing in Wales, had decided to take in one of the great tourist attractions of the area. With over a hundred others, he traveled to the top of Mt. Snowden where he stood expectantly waiting for a glorious sunrise. He wasn't disappointed. The sun rose over the peak of the mountain, and its beautiful rays filled the valleys below with sheer glory. Dr. Hall was overwhelmed. At first, he couldn't speak, and then gradually he felt moved to pour out his heart in prayer. As he lifted his voice to God, tears rolled down the faces of the people, and a sweet silent calm seemed to descend on each one. Then quietly, with awe, they moved down the mountain and went their own ways.

Sometime later Dr. Hall was informed by a local pastor of the conversion of forty people on the mountain that morning. It seemed they had all joined the local church. "But," said Dr. Hall, "all I did was pray."

"Yes," the pastor replied, "and more wonderful still is the fact that they didn't understand a word you said, for you spoke English and they are Welsh." [2]

Dr. Hall learned something very important that day. He learned that the Spirit's cry from within was even more powerful than the emotional gratitude he felt as he surveyed God's wonders that morning on the mountain. God answered the deepest desire of Dr. Hall's heart . . . that of hungering for souls to enter God's kingdom. He took a simple prayer of gratitude and refashioned it to win souls. What a privilege! We pray

---

[2] Paul Lee Tan, ThD, "Newman Hall Didn't Preach," in *Signs of the Times, Encyclopedia of 77,000 Illustrations*, (Rockville, MD: Assurance Publishers) 1430.

to a loving Father who transforms our prayers into the highest good.

Dr. Hall's prayer of worship was answered, but certainly not as he would have expected. The same is true of so many of our prayers. We think we are praying for one thing, yet God is reading the heart behind the prayer.

For just such a reason as this, it is important that we not fashion what we think should be the answer to any prayer. It is enough to know that God answers all the prayers of His children.

"The eyes of the Lord are on the righteous, and His ears are open to their cries" (Psalm 34:15 NKJV).

"He shall call upon Me, and I will answer him" (Psalm 91:15 NKJV).

"Until now you have asked nothing in my name. Ask and you will receive" (John 16:24 NKJV).

"And whatever things you ask in prayer, believing, you will receive" (Matthew 21:22 NKJV).

Remember, for some the answer may be, "Not yet My child," or "It would not be wisdom for Me to give this to you." For others, a response from God might simply be, "Yes." Whichever the case may be, we can be certain no prayer will go unanswered.

My heart recalls one answer to prayer that fell into the "not yet" category. When I heard this story it impacted my heart in such a way that I have never forgotten it.

When Robert Moffat, Scottish missionary to South Africa, prayerfully returned to recruit helpers in his homeland, he was greeted by the fury of a cold British winter. Arriving at the church where he was to speak, he was disturbed to note that only a small group of ladies had braved the elements to hear his message based on, *"Unto you, O men, I call"* (Proverbs 8:4 KJV). Moffat felt hopeless as he gave the appeal, realizing that few women could be expected to undergo the rigorous experiences they would face in the jungles where he labored. But God works in mysterious ways to carry out His wise purposes.

In his consternation Moffat failed to notice one boy in the loft who had come to work the bellows of the organ. This young fellow was thrilled by Moffat's challenge. Deciding that he would follow in the footsteps of this pioneer missionary, he went to school, obtained a degree in medicine, and then spent the rest of his life ministering to the unreached tribes of Africa. His name: Dr. David Livingston! God gave the missionary an answer that was far greater than his request. Much later in Moffat's life he discovered what God had brought forth on that one disappointing night . . . the greatest medical missionary to ever set foot on the soil of Africa. He did so by calling a boy in a church where Robert Moffat felt his prayers for help had gone unanswered.[3]

Yes, God answers all of His children's prayers. Often not instantly or in the way we would imagine, but He faithfully answers our prayers, often exceeding our requests.

[3] Paul Lee Tan, ThD, "Newman Hall Didn't Preach," in *Signs of the Times, Encyclopedia of 77,000 Illustrations*, (Rockville, MD: Assurance Publishers) 482.

BECOMING PRAYER

F ew of us have ever heard the term "becoming prayer." It almost seems otherworldly, a work that occurs when we get to heaven. However, I believe it is a principle that God longs to work into our lives while we are yet earthbound.

What does "becoming prayer" really mean, and how is it possible to rest in prayer when prayer is an action that could appear to cause such striving? For this we need to look into God's Word.

Christians have puzzled and overwhelmed for years over 1 Thessalonians 5:17:

"Pray without ceasing" (KJV, NKJV, NAS).

"Pray continually" (NIV).

"Pray all the time" (MSG).

Most believers look at this verse and say, "That is impossible. God asks too much." However, as God has drawn me into the prayers of His heart, I have come to believe that it is not only possible, but that praying without ceasing ultimately transforms us into prayer itself. We literally *become prayer*. Our problem, I think, is that we don't rightly define *prayer* in this passage. Most of us imagine that praying without ceasing is to mutter words to God constantly, and, yes, that is virtually impossible.

Becoming prayer begins with God's sovereignty.

First, we must see God's hand in everything (see Chapter 1). From the smallest thing to the greatest, from the most insignificant to the most overpowering, from the most joyful to the most painful . . . all are either allowed or brought to us through a sovereign Father. When our heart responds with, "Somehow God is using this in my life," we have taken our first step toward becoming prayer.

Next, we see that our reactions to life can become worship (see Chapter 2). Worship is one of the highest forms of prayer, and when worship permeates our responses to the issues of life, we are becoming prayer. Even when we are fully focused on the work we are given in this world, living in an attitude that says, "All of this is from God, through God, and to God" helps us to become prayer.

When we read Scripture and respond to what we read by asking God to make that Word real within us and to work it out in our lives, we are responding to

God and we are becoming prayer. When we allow God's Word to break our hearts with the knowledge of some revealed failing so that we come to Him for forgiveness, we are becoming prayer.

After recognizing God in every facet and movement in life, and learning to worship Him with our responses, then we must take a close look at the 17th chapter of John where Jesus prays for His followers:

"My prayer is not for them alone. I pray also for those who will believe in Me through their message, that all of them may be one, Father, just as You are in Me and I am in You. May they also be in Us so that the world may believe that You have sent Me? I have given them the glory that You gave Me, that they may be one as We are one: I in them and You in Me. May they be brought to complete unity to let the world know that You sent Me and have loved them even as You have loved Me" (John 17:20–23 NIV).

Through the glory that was given us by Christ, through the cross, we are empowered to become one with each other and one with our Lord. Because the Father indwells Christ, when the Lord comes to live in us, He brings the Father to live there as well. Clearly, we become the prayer of Christ and His answered prayer when we *"become one with each other and one with our God."* This oneness creates the place for God in our hearts that enables us to hear how He might have us pray.

Longing for this unhindered flow of unity is a critical part of becoming prayer. Perhaps this helps us to understand why relationship with God is so important. Out of that relationship, oneness flows, and out of oneness our hearts become more and more aware of God's prayers rather than our own. Longing for and seeking oneness with each other and with our God fosters our becoming prayer. But even this is not about working something up inside in order to achieve a new way of life; it is about heart–set.

Although you can't *make* this prayer life happen, you *can* open your arms and your heart wide, asking the Father to bring it to pass. Ask Him for a better way and tell Him that you are willing to put away all the old regimented approaches to prayer. Humble your heart before Him and ask for that which He longs to give you . . . the transition from just simply *saying prayer*, to actually *becoming prayer*. It is a gift He would desire for each one of us. How it pleases Him for us to ask!

Many Christians have been crying out to God,

saying, "There has to be something more." Becoming prayer is a part of that "something more." It is a call to come up higher, to live above the circumstances of life, and to no longer be drawn in and dragged down by what is happening around us. There is a rest in God that is available to all of us right here on planet earth.

"Are you tired? Worn out? Burned out on religion? Come to Me. Get away with Me and you'll recover your life. I'll show you how to take a real rest. Walk with Me and work with Me—watch how I do it. Learn the unforced rhythms of grace. I won't lay anything heavy or ill–fitting on you. Keep company with Me and you'll learn to live freely and lightly" (Matthew 11:28–30 MSG).

The *"unforced rhythms of grace"* call us to a life of becoming prayer. It's not a life requiring our striving, but rather simple openness, a longing heart, and a desire to enter the place of *rest* called *prayer*.

For those who are hearing this call for the very first time, I say, "Your time with the Lord is about to take on a whole new meaning, with a greater dimension of peace in prayer than you have ever known." And for *all* who hunger for a new place in God, I say, "**Welcome. Welcome to the Heart of Prayer**."

Faith is not a feeling;
it is action. It is
a willed choice.

ELISABETH ELLIOT

*You need not cry very
loud; He is nearer to
us than we think.*

BROTHER LAWRENCE

As I finish this book on prayer, I am drawn to share another beautiful picture of personal sovereignty that God has shown me. I was surprised when the Lord began speaking to me again about the issue of sovereignty, for He had already said so much. How could there be more? However, this explanation gave me a visual understanding, for He knew my human, finite mind needed a simple way to grasp the working of His sovereignty in *my own personal life.*

I believe this new understanding will change my life, so I cannot leave the subject of prayer without offering His words to you, and praying they will touch your heart even as they have already begun to touch my own.

First, He showed me a plate that was prepared for each of us before our birth. The plate held just the right amounts of joy and sorrow, of happiness and pain, and of struggle and rest. All of which, carefully measured and balanced, were apportioned to us before we came into this world.

He also spoke to my spirit of the actual plate that holds all of these issues of our lives. He explained that the plate itself is made of four elements. First, it holds the prayers we would pray concerning all we would one day long to be in Him (He knew the end from the beginning). Second, the plate is made of what *He* desired for us to be during our life on this earth. And the third and forth components of the plate are His two promises, *"I will accomplish what concerns you"* (paraphrase of Psalm 138:8) and *"I will complete the work I have begun in you"* (Philippians 1:6 NAS). In essence, the foundation of all of these carefully measured seasons and moments of life are based on our prayers, God's desire for us, and God's promises to us.

At first I thought, "Does this mean we don't do our best to wisely avoid what appears to be destructive situations?" His reply was, "Of course not. But it does mean that *when there is nothing more you can do concerning a situation*, you release it all to Me, who with love and mercy balances all things well in your life."

*All God desires for
you to be in this life.*

*All He knew you would
pray to be in Him.*

*His promise, "I will
accomplish what
concerns you."*

*His promise, "I will
complete the work I have
begun in you."*

With this revelation, I was reminded me of the
song *It is Well With My Soul*, which was written by
Horatio Spafford. Here was a man who had lost his
possessions, his business, and his infant son. Within a
matter of weeks the rest of His children, three young
daughters, died suddenly when the ship on which they
were traveling to England sank in the Atlantic. In one
line of the song the grieving Spafford writes, *"Whatever
my lot, Thou hast taught me to say, 'It is well, it is well with
my soul.'"*

The "lot" about which Spafford wrote, God explained to me, was the "plate" of which He had spoken. I then began to understand what the Father was teaching me about His sovereignty in my personal life.

Next, He answered another question of my heart before I even had a chance to ask it. I had always stopped short of abandoning myself to the Lord for fear that *more* struggles or suffering would come. He helped me understand that fully abandoning ourselves to Him would not bring more pain or sorrow to our plates, because our willingness to give ourselves totally to Him does not change what has been placed there. However, such self–abandon does change the heart of the person holding the plate, and a heart so changed is one He delights to display before men.

Those who have experienced such a heart–change have stepped into the Lord's call to "take up your cross and follow Me." We don't have to ask the Lord to bring us a cross or go looking for one so we can do as He asked—*the cross is already on the plate we were given.* The question now becomes, "Will you take it up with a new heart–set and follow Me?"

I asked the Lord what it would look like to

embrace the portion of the plate that represents the cross in our lives, and the Spirit told me:

"When you find yourself walking through the struggles, pain, sorrows, or loss—which are a part of the plate you have been given—I would have you acknowledge My presence by *thanking Me for trusting you with an experience you may not be able to understand this side of heaven.* In so praying, you worship Me, you honor your Father in the midst of your pain, and you walk in the steps of your Savior. Your heart–cry has become, 'Not my will but Thy will be done.' How could there ever be a prayer more pleasing to the heart of your God?"

Perhaps it is appropriate that we end this book with a life–changing look at sovereignty because that is where we began so many pages ago. How fitting it seems, for the topic is much like the cover of a book that holds all the pages together.

Praise God, He reigns! His sovereign love and power rule over the world that whirls about us and over each of our individual lives—each uniquely blessed journey toward heaven. I don't know about you, but understanding that truth about sovereignty gives me a level of peace and rest that can't be found on this earth apart from Him.

My prayers are deeply affected by the sovereignty of my God, for it frees me in a whole new way to enter into His rest. All of my foolish striving disappears, and I fall, with abandonment, into the arms of my Lord, asking Him how to pray, listening for His heart, and trusting Him with the answers. His pure, unchanging love treasures every word and answers my requests based on His infinite knowledge of all that is best for me and for those I love. What a wonderful place of quiet rest . . . the heart of prayer. Will you join me there?

Trust the past to God's mercy, the present to God's love, and the future to God's providence.

ST. AUGUSTINE

CONTINUING THE JOURNEY

If *The Heart of Prayer* has been meaningful for you, you also might like:

The Women of Faith Prayer Journal, by Lana Bateman

Go deeper into the Heart of Prayer with this forty-day guided journal.

Irrepressible Hope: Devotions to Anchor Your Soul and Buoy Your Spirit, by Patsy Clairmont, Barbara Johnson, Nicole Johnson, Marilyn Meberg, Luci Swindoll, and Thelma Wells

The core team of Women of Faith shares sixty devotions of how irrepressible hope has enriched their lives, strengthened their relationships with the Savior, and kept them afloat when circumstances threatened to pull them under.

Keeping a Princess Heart, by Nicole Johnson

This is a thoughtful exploration of the tension women feel between what they long for and what they live with in this not so fairy tale world.

WOMEN OF FAITH MISSION STATEMENT

Women of Faith wants all women to know God loves them unconditionally, no matter what. The ministry reaches out through motivational, yet moving conferences. Since 1996, more than 2,000,000 women have attended Women of Faith events in dozens of cities across North America.

Women of Faith is a nondenominational women's ministry committed to helping women of all faiths, backgrounds, age groups, and nationalities be set free to a lifestyle of God's grace. Founded specifically to meet the needs to women, Women of Faith is committed to nurturing women spiritually, emotionally, and relationally—whether it be in marriages, friendships, the workplace, or with their children. Our goal is to provide hope and encouragement in all areas of life, especially those that can wear women down and steal their joy and hope.

Women of Faith, which has become America's largest women's conference, exists to deliver great news to women: God loves them, and there are a bunch of girlfriends out there who love them, too! Through laughter, music, dramas, and gut-level, real-life stories about how God has worked through the good and bad of our lives, Women of Faith reminds women that God is crazy about them!

For more information or to register
for a conference, please visit
www.womenoffaith.com

or call
1-888-49-FAITH